word*sword*

Dear Joan,

Thanks for
bringing art
to life.

Doorword

A number of the poems in this volume have been shaped by what will be called "quantum poetry." The premise that we're quantum beings—psychologically as well as physically—isn't altogether new, having been considered by authors such as Amit Goswami, Fred Alan Wolf and others.

The definition of "quantum nature" is many splendored, quixotic, and not wholly understood by any person. Technical details of this question will be left to the reader's present knowledge and future research. It's not the intention of this form or forum of verse to engage in physics, but to treat human nature from a certain perspective.

In general, however, these are some of the basic quantum phenomena involved:

• complementarity – Though impossible from the standpoint of classical physics, subatomic particles exhibit characteristics of either matter or of waves, depending on the design of the experiment.

• quantized action – In the quantum domain, energy is emitted and absorbed in discrete and particular quantities or "quanta," not in a continuous flow or in irregular quantities.

• transmigration – With absorption or emission of energy, electrons relocate to higher or lower shells around an atomic nucleus, but they don't traverse the space between; they simply disappear from one shell and reappear on the other.

• Uncertainty Principle – The more precisely a subatomic particle's motion is measured, the less its position can be ascertained, and vice versa, presenting a persisting ambiguity.

• memory of interaction – Particles which interact will remain sensitive to each other despite distance or time.

• nonlocality – Synchronous action of particles at a distance indicates a signal system faster than the speed of light, exceeding this presumed limit.

The reader can be assured, while knowledge of quantum mechanics ought to enhance the reading of this work, these poems can be expected to stand in lieu of such knowledge.

We have so much yet to learn about the nature of reality—the reality of nature—particularly in the phenomenal areas that have been most shunned. These quantum effects aren't anomalous, but the status quo in the physical world.

There can be no classical description for the quantum mind; we'd seem to need a quantum language. The poetics here imagines that concepts and their symbology retain the qualities of those objects and conditions represented, that verbal language carries a quantum potential.

For example, in the infinite field of possible meanings, concepts exist in "superposition." The field's collapse, to a set of concepts forming a thought, can be likened to the collapse of the wave function in an experimental framework.

Conscious of our quantum condition, the writer can accentuate this with devices of language. For example, "Heartpouring" (page 9) comments on friendship at a distance by alluding to the phenomenon of nonlocality.

Like quantum space, concept matrices can be seen as holographic domains. Any concept or quantum vantage point is a "room full of doors." The metaphysical view of this poetics far exceeds what's condoned by the scientific canon. Poetry is the grandfather of science, the secret lover of science, and the child who plays on the swingset of science.

The pieces in the book which were written consciously as quantum poems have a q as a designation in the date.

LZS

Dedicated to
Cheryl Lynn Faulkner

wordsword

an excursion in quantum poetry

by Zach Shatz

PRISMIND
PUBLICATIONS
P.O. Box 11635
Berkeley CA 94712

Other books by Zach Shatz:

Prisms and Mind
Time is a Broken Carafe
Simple Season of the Will

ISBN 1-892814-25-0

Library of Congress Control Number: 2002109767

Silver falls from leaves.
The drops make coins on the ground.
Blades reach to claim them.

1995

quanta of ideas
are nothing^2 compared
to quanta of faces

it's the faces that throw light
and ideas that go chasing after

2001*q*

the space of the page
has been rearranged
to cast light
and catch shade
these cubes of ideas
and tetrahedral dreams
projecting
icosahedral fields
reflecting
around the reader
verbal contours of geometry

1997*q*

Flip the Light Fantastic

Angels visiting
don't make much trouble
even know where the light switch is.
Funny though, they might flip it
back again forth again only gets brighter.
They keep flipping, gets so bright
I can't see anymore
have to feel my way through.
They're really not much trouble
bearing delicacies on the wing
a nouvelle entree, something called manna
sweet to the taste, light on the waist
makes me hungrier and hungrier, yet satisfied.
Not much trouble I have to say
these angels with their party ways
    jumping into each new note
    weaving of sounds reflective chords
    that flow like scenes in streams.

1995q

Three Dogs Dreaming

Three dogs went down to sleep at night.
One dreamt of love, two dreamt of fright.
Three dogs in each dream wandered down the road
    in three reals seeming, reels of roles.

The three that walked in the thought of love
all shared that space, moved in time
    fell together in a fold.

Those caught in dreams beckoned by fright
forsaking one another, moved in strife
    fell to pieces split by cold.

Three great birds make gliding turns
loop and race onward, wings pushing sky,
three paths' cavortings interweaving
    entwined, one flight, communion.

Two groups of rivals with sharpened swords
make battle to act out a script of discord,
cutting with attitudes ribbons of blood
    blades' edges dueling, what's mine or yours.

Each dog awakens to a different world,
one canine's healed, two've been gored.
    In unity all thrive, by attitudes are torn,
    in light fear is fleeting, on edge love is gone.

1995*q*

Let the Wind Blow

Never in all the world
has there ever stood
any unchanging thing
    just a firmer clay.

No rock has escaped time
immortal is no rhyme
the flowers come and go
they're waving so you'll know
with hellos come goodbyes
no point in asking why
    just say hello.

Eternally is there one
abiding con/s/ver/v/sation
the tower of today
will be as yesterday
    our hallowed ground.

Never in all the world
has any stone withstood
the flames of rain and wind
    all goes wood's way.

No rock has escaped time
a diamond will unbind
by forces bending proofs
no point protecting truths
that hold us in their spell
verities protect themselves
    just let the wind blow.

The babe is but a rock
unto the elements
insisting by its grain
a part of now to claim
    takes shape its heart.

1999q

Ode to the Bee

There's no better buzzer than the bee.
And the buzz is better the busier the bee.
Wouldn't you be buzzing
if your business was nectar collector?
What a job! The bee was not upset
when informed, "For the rest of your days
you must take flight and visit every flower."
So satisfied is the bee with its lot in life
it builds temples of hexagons
and tithes with honey.
    When life is sweet
    being busy is a buzz
    and it's great just bee-ing.

1997*q*

Heartpouring

Because we're alone only if
we choose.
Nothing's gone
when we give of ourselves
into hands our own anyway
    the infinite a fidelity,
like hitchhikers headed home
stick out our necks and go
    arriving at an end
    in being where we've been,
goodbyes not leaving but believing
at home we're not alone,
no distance between friends.
On the soul's path
our oneness ever lasts,
distance is a fiction
and the heart can't read,
what's lost isn't real
in the conservation of mystery.
No one loses themselves
who makes wholeness in giving,
    a ride that has an end
    is every whole's beginning.
In goodbyes we hold our friends.

1997q

Sweet is not big or small but fine
like fields of wild grass
the fullness
    described, is not full.

Joy is not big or small but warm
like crystal goblet's contents
an enchantment
    named, is not charm.

Song is not big or small but soothing
like curves of a winding path
the flow
    defined, is not free.

The sweet joy of song is not big or small.
It is you.

The Size of the Sphere

some stories can't help being poems
by the paths they forge into the depths
and then we know the nature of poem
where meanings ripple outward forever
the beat of a thought sounding
    of the One sound

the night sky is as land seen from a boat
the constellations buildings, ancient architectures
distant shores fixed in relative space
their movement tells our own movement
the boat, our world,
    slowly parts the waters of the Way

if we listen with our eyes to the starry sky
very closely listen we can see
the Earth's actual turning, boat against land
then by Circadian sense of day's length
can fit this motion with the telling of time
and by calculations intuitive, see
from the simple spot on which we stand
    with our own eyes
    the size of the sphere

1999q

*SHORT ORDER POETRY; custom written
on the spot by Mike Holland in Sonoma, CA,
in answer to the question:*

What's at the End of the Rainbow?

Rainbows that I've seen
don't end, I've tried
many times to find them.
They're either fake
or they move too fast.
I've run after them,
ridden bicycles, horses,
rollerskates, and only
once did I find even
the most ragged remnants
of color hanging
from a barbed wire fence.

7/30/96

<u>Fork in the Frame</u>

    Which way
do I feel
I'm of the world
servant or master
    part of it
    or all that it is
what right have I
and what then is left
    to take the glory
    or waken to it
in each frame
the fork persists
this story's gates
my choices ink
    ever flowing
    downhill
(even metaphor is forked
when voices have choices)

what's right
and what's left
tells good and evil
my part becomes
    a frame full filled
or a loathesome whole
    hogging the picture
which way do I feel
I'm of the story
    life of the party
    or party to life
in my wholeness
am I consumed
    taken with myself
or awake unto it
    humbled before glory
fates bifurcate
ink's gates are opened

a path taken
    is all that it is
a path ventured
    walks in greater grace
which way do I feel
I AM a story
    divine being an icon
    or being a rivulet
which carries me farther
    transcending above
    or into the one
is reality my own making
or a landscape of revelation
in the frame lays my fate
a story to create
as master or servant
    one path bent on taking
    one a curve ever waiting.

2000*q*

Mraz Space

He sang, or was he
pouring ambrosia from his heart
I learned of the moment
feared for its passing
I'd never known
a man could sing, sing, sing.
    In the headlights of a tone
    trapped in a voice grip
    a butterfly held me down
    nothing but wings and
    joy tore free.

Baby Waves

From deep inside greater waves
pop out the baby waves
    crawling up the shore
grains of sand the crystals
of babies' first tears

but this misses too much
regarding these babies

From deep inside greater waves
unfold thoughts newborn
rolling into youth
bold adolescence rising
into that face of a wave
then reaching and falling innocence
wrestles churning adulthood
struggles to keep its head up
fights on making a wave for itself
gives all it's got in the crossroads of fate
scrambles home, ambling
for a comfortable resting place
sighs gushing on the shore

here come the babies
    returning.

1996

wordsword

to the Institute of Noetic Sciences

Perfection is a Rhythm

Walk on the line and never see the circle.
Measure time and never know the day.
Be washed clean but the spring's not sterile.
Build upon life but leave the sky free.
Writing is a winged thing,
    flight spilling from a feather.
Happy is the one who is riding on the wind.
Believe in the mind and listen to its rhythm.
Understand nature's perfection within.

The line is illusion, the circle God's kingdom;
embracing the line leaves the hands tied.
Time is a mystery no one can decipher;
like an infant in a mother's arms, so are we in time.
Clean is the dirt from which life has arisen;
sterile is the fear the earth is not the truth.
Our world can be built up to further life's purpose;
piling desks in the sky does few any service.
The capacity to write is a ticket to adventure;
when words take to striding, meaning's waylaid.
A kite is symbolic of happiness and freedom;
anchored to the ground yet flutters of its own.
The mind is musical, a medley of vibrations;
rhythms we must find or will drown in the sound.
Nature is the miracle of change charged with order;
the concept of perfection a unicycle ride.

1995q

Thoughts of Goethe

To see the truth, to see the light
I well up with profound delight
that knowing is an eye's partaking,
all is found participating.
Listening is the highest practice
in the flow spirit relaxes,
knowledge is a changing thing
and to One mind your own must bring.
I find my heart is growing full
as thoughts combine to make me whole
where pieces piled just seem as stuff
all pieced together picture love.
So as I live and each next day
my open mind is all that stays.

to Riki Shatz and Roxc Ornelas
on the occasion of their wedding

On your special day
        may puffs of clouds
bring their imagery
        into attendance,
the southern California sun
        paint those images
spectacular.

May the East and West
        and North and South
be present to send you
        centered to the heart
where you and your other
        dance in all directions.

May no masks
        ever come between you
but those painted
        for beauty.

1994

DeCarbo

Through mists the hills of years
rise and roll away
quietly, echoing memories
of tales told taller, revelling
ennobled minds aspiring
horizons golden, forests gleam
and the birds trill
like the dawn of dawns
and the sun is God's mind
and this kingdom is all storied.
So is DeCarbo queen of the day
in whose hours live myth and legend.

The sun's rays, streaming threads
remind me of your hair
    flowing all fire, rarified.
To gaze in the flood of light
feeds the generation
    of root's deep driving energy.
The source of this heaven sent
is brilliant in your eyes
    and warmly is contained.
Your beaming love of life
strikes the leaves of my mind
    and by a synthesis fetes me.

The time is telling
All Awake!
that sleep should not our aspirations
    confiscate
shelved upon nighttime's repast
wishes trapped on a story's page,
the coins for their release
spent in throes to lesser wells
leaving the fortune of fable's fate
    to drown
in quiet between paper sheets
    laid down.

The time is telling
All Awake!
to walk into the blazing day
the truth is born each step we take
no rules or roles or promises
    but these we make
to shape the wandering's journey
wondering our way to the sea
    and the seeing
a journey's way a journey's name
the fable unfolding ceaselessly
portraying ourselves each page
    we choose
the turning leaves, the colored tale,
    the living tree.

1999

Madonna

It's not because your hair is full
    and that your skin is so lovely,

that you live your life responsibly
    and keep ahead of this world,

or that you know how to heal
    or how to communicate

or that you understand so well
    the importance of each one's opinion
of the democrats and republicans
of the rich and the poor
of the women and the men,
    so fair are you.

It's that God shines so strongly through you
and by this passage brings grace to my eyes
that your smile carries the life
    of your Maker, and mine.

It's the hugs you give to friends
and the time you have for everyone
which remind me of the ways
  of the Lord.

It's the Light that brightens your hair
  the Life glowing upon your skin,
the Light that is ever responsible
  as the Lamp of this world.

Who is the Healer?
Who makes all things known?
Where derives the agent of such patient listening?

I tell you that I love you
but not so often as you show me
God is always there.

1995

You are the sun's rays
You are the forest bed
You are the picture in a cloud
You are the hands and feet;

You are the scent of pine
You are the babbling brook
You are the concert violin
You are the spinning Earth;

You are the road paved with gold
You are the yellow brick road
You are the yellow ribbon 'round the old oak tree
You are the future's gifts;

You are the bolt of alabaster silk
You are the hydrofoil
You are the space-based telescope
You are the World Cup;

You are the antique book
You are the sound of drums
You are the taste of rain
You are my Everything.

Plagued by hopes
stars only light my tears,
the sparkles of a crown
I hold with empty hands
the only dream worth dreaming
my heart does not fail.
The streets at night
these days and hours
the way, concrete aglitter
every step made hostage
to vain prayers leading me
my heart does not fail.
Quiet finds passing
yearnings in a gait
my carriage two humble feet
toward what destiny
God would speak
my heart does not fail.
The dawn is grace
faith's gifts bestowed
raising gilded palaces
works reveal the soul
love the kingdom's curtain
my heart does not fail.
It dies for you.

1996

Door of a Bad Thing

There's a thrill of feeling
like I just broke through
the door of a bad thing
with no power to hurt me
    only sidewayslike
    as it hurts itself.
That's the nature of the Beast.
It swings so hard and reckless
the arm whiffing by, striking out
    at its pain.
The bad thing is the hurt
kept from the light.
The door of a bad thing
has a broken hinge
and won't stay tight.

Enjoy It

Life is a lion
claws razor sharp
and a roar frighteningly loud
its saliva hot and thick
on your upper body and neck
its teeth made to devour you.
Let it.

When its bite finds your soft parts
jaw swiftly ripping your flesh
passionately it loves you, delights in you.
You were made to be devoured.

Let the lion take you in its mighty mouth,
proudly it eats you, choice and juicy,
as a meal more alive than ever in your life.

The lion is real
musculature insurmountable
stomach inescapable.
Be in love with the lion as it is with you
or you will taste sour.
Be in love and allow that life devours.

1994

Take Your Hand Away

I was there for a year
the guy was
everything *so* close to the chest
including his crude jokes
room was big rent was low
beautiful views of the sky
raking his yard, scrubbing his tub
child running by
then a lookalike
just as much a child
    only bigger
with tantrums to match.

Water's shut off, 'lectricity's not paid
I pay it for him, tell him cash the same day
he stops with a look like I gave 'im a hook
I says "you live alone? go flake away
but as a landlord, don't tread on me"
"How dare you talk that way to me
in my own house!"
    he said quietly
    as he lept from the couch
    across the room grabbing me
    ripping my shirt by the neck.
You're a big boy now
be a man
take your hand away.

Victorious Secret

Big balls of boob
bounce off my eyes
thrown by a picture
advertising brassieres
heaving soft cleavage
onto the world
smothered happy
crushed gleeful
buried jubilant
choked on joy
gasping and grabbing

fullness of silken skin
pumping victoriously
claiming all who behold it
desire humbled by grace
might stayed by mammaries
the cuckoo's treasure chest
miraculous like water
a bounty of precious abundance
this milk for growing bones
sold so would sour
only beauty beyond price
sustains the image's power.

1999

Our capacity for free will is at the same time
our fear of disconnection, for in free will
is the individual, unto oneself, taking risks.
Then action, the expression of our free will,
is a source of fear. This fear is pierced
by our awareness that in action, and individuality,
we're being our part of the greater field;
we're not disconnecting but finding connection.
It is in this very awareness that we find
the glory of the Divinity within us, the Self.

And when you believe someone
has nothing to offer you,
your belief will make it true,
and when you believe someone
can give you something by virtue
of your differences, then
you will find a greater truth.
The highest spiritual act
is *listening*. In this we are open
to the unknowns of the world
and to the unknowns
within ourselves.

Confiding to me the man said
we're all wild animals in our cages
pitched with rage bouncing off the bars
the Destroyer inside, I heard him say,
is afraid that he might get free.

Oh I said casually eyeing the door latch
what makes him mad I said and he said nothing
made him mad he clenched and spit a little.

Oh I said even caged birds get restless
I thought let's be glad for cages I said
even a bird free of the cage flies
to what it needs, even for birds
being free isn't the end of it.

He growled and half-knowing shook the wheel.

1996

What if a Poet

What if a poet
said it to show it
in words of ideas from his heart
set off like fireworks

a flashy symphony
a line epiphany
the poem mystery

words going off in the dark

float swimmingly, casting imagery
enfolding reflections' synergy
composing meaning's euphony

of words of ideas of his singing heart.

1997q

What is Realized

The figure springs through shapes of space
looking divertedly as if traversing a garden,
slants of light cut by edges' meetings
seconds' faces overlapping
        rearranging time.

The figure finds itself in reflection
coming around corners to open place of self
into possibility in an air of action
        —once again letting go of the side.

The figure flies into colors' parade
folds in with compounding tapestries
pieces of geometry interiorized
and in metamorphism's fruit
        majesterialized.

1997q

Web of Agreement

Light into the pool dives down
playings writ on container's ground
facets swimming tight and loose
characters all free and bound
the staging of a tale knit under
quantas' viscous overcoat
the morphing liquid
shadow of waves beneath.

Then aflight in dreamspell
sweeping birds the pattern keep
beyond sciences competing
all forms in agreement
a bird brained winking of wisdom
intelligence transmind
nature shows a wit
in woven choreographies.

In the pool, the sky, the dream
a magnetic paradigm
poles interlocking easily
tight and loose, holding and heaving
the whole
a madness of coordination
One still and never ceasing
in eyes mesmerized.

Watery is the story
mystique upon the wall
webscape's echoed harmony
geometry's motion spins mystery
space now meeting infinitely
a Song of choral being.

2000q

Crafty Mother

She played classical
        in the next room
to teach them unawares
    with good things
distance and thought aren't factors
    for a listening heart
        don't mistake
children for anything else.

A faint spell like the stars and moon
        wafting
    as from a far off
        mountain crater
    as from the Earth's center,
Mozart courses into the child's soul.
    The feeding, aurally,
of the soft garden soil
        of the growing mind
builds cathedrals within
        to savor sounds unheard.

to Angie and Todd Soares
on the occasion of their wedding

Hunger has a source so deep
it hunts and chews as we sleep.
Humans have a soul to feed
the heart does pump but for a need.
The table set is dreaming's art
but what is served is living's part.
Out of the dream into the day
we fill the plate by how we play.
Life becomes a dream fulfilled
when playing leaves the palate thrilled.
Back in sleep the meal digests
and the hunger of the heart has rest.
By the candle lit with love, Grace pray,
    then lick the spoon, drink Beaujolais.

2000

The Mystery of Christmas

When young Sean now lept upon
    the gift-wrapped boxes waiting there
in all their colors, bows and charm
he left this world to enter on
    the magic of a Christmas Day,
so long he'd suffered impatiently
to know this stuff 'twas all tied up
    beneath long boughs of evergreen.

Unto the life of a child's heart
    he jumped and danced with zeal
and settled down to meddle with all
    these fantasies he'd made,
never looked he up to see
    the treetop's glitt'ring angel.

From her perch she watched him
  and lifted her, adulation,
to feel the fire flamed so high
  from the eyes a smile cradled.
The angel flew and heavenward
  with the gift of man to God
news announced in halls on high
  of a joy oft fabled.

The one who died to give us life
wins his wish in wonder's breath,
yet warm inside the family home
  the story of old descries
innocence plays indifferent
  to the miraculous bequest.

1995

Shape of Essence

spirit
Bounced off a moon
of an astral celestiality
your face is that reflection
shadowy with moondust,
birth from the womb of heaven
there you are a beam of light.

soul
Within the light there play three hues
whose combinatings color you
these three match up in seven ways
the seven chakras sit for *qi*
emotions tell the chakras' flow
the heart the store of energies' journeys.

mind
These combinatings, harnessed, pay
the orderly from the arbitrary weighs
by compositings destinies are built
following designs of imagining
and life becomes an escapade
of being Creators.

will
is gold mined at the heights of a highrise?
does power lead to love?
do we seriously think we command anything?
who goes beyond what nature allows?
what rules should we choose?
what stories will our hearts record?

1999q

I was home after work
listening to the radio report
the news guy said *traffic:*
Hot? Vallejo! CalTrans is repairing
the road buckled from the heat
accident 80 interchange with 580 east
hopeless situation Bay Bridge lower deck.
I remembered my ride home on BART
how peaceful it was.

Lady letter carrier
working from door to door
white sun helmet bobbing
and dressed like a stamp delivering
little ones on sheath surfaces
containing the honey drop
      of information.

to Julia Vinograd

Window Poetry

Stopped for the light
I look to the right
window is sudden cinema
just there on screen a woman
buoyed by a parking meter
face hunkered down tight
in black robes, velvet cap
a poet I deeply respect up close
scans the avenue contemplating
the next horizon, course of verse.
A glow emanating from her interior
lights and softens round features
telling of hope determinedly new
her gaze clear as a sea captain's
taking measure of the currents
picking out by experience and soul
what captain's mates might not detect
and in her glances castigation
from a deep love
not willing to accept what's seen.

2001

The Past

History is a crucible of pain
one country overrunning another
one leader overpowering another
one neighbor neglecting another
one of the family betraying another
killers and rapists and thieves and tyrants
brutality, injustice and domination,
the record a fit of agony.

We're reminded of great moments
of nobility, virtue and kindness,
these acts of love, these glimpses
of what the human might be
are lip service in a paean of history,
      homilies of the warmth of home
      turn hot in mind of secret abominations.

We have reminiscences of cultures
displaying valor our species has destroyed.

Oh, America

It's a craft
called Glory
the US flagship
destination freedom
no mouth too small
to be heard
or fed promises
the dream
once was great
to every citizen
one's own slate
dissent renewal
a cooperative whole
protection
for personality
rainbow's fruition
that bridge
for wishing.

A craft
sales buffeted
by gluttony
sour winds
warped dreams
not one for all
but for none other
rogue destination
of loudmouths
dissent not decent
cents the only
sense, flagrant
scent's fragrance
beauty half-price
protection
skewed to despoil
fruition
a hollow core.

A craft
shining, flag flying
promises celluloid
the frame melting
freedom aflame
one wish, one slate
all mouths herded
destination currency
rainbows portfolios
the nation's cooperation
a golf game
with clubs for the few
personality
a putting green
a tidy course
down the drain
this painted ship
a rotting folly
reeks and wrecks.

2000

'Cause

seek what you can dream
reach for all you imagine
'cause nothing will be lost
in taking time for play

look for your dreams
'cause they're looking for you
look for your dreams
if you wish them to come true

dream of your dreams
'cause they've been dreaming of you

Soup of the Day

The parts availed of a child's mind
need only be made moving
that moves them has meaning...
enscripting a tale of dream's weaving
so the heart stays strong.
What's moving consumes them
chasing the tail of their own making,
    parts stirred consomme.

Heart Teaching

The sages say, "follow your heart"
lit within stillness is the good path
in feelings flow the promise of treasure
hope the well of beneficence

moved by images of our wishing
honor guides turns of decision
there lays surprise beyond this mirage
the living waters of Divine desire

love is the end, we return to beginnings
the discovery that birth is destiny
each moment we live emerges newborn
in love youth springs eternal

delights of life cannot be caught
choice finds its way in imagining
image to follow, mirage to pierce, love to discover
in the quieted mind rises the glory road

from hopes come surgings of the heart
a soul that's fed feels its form
shape is image, entrancing is dancing
flowing feelings glowing gold.

1999q

Make it So

Make it so all eyes have met
to know each other soul to soul
until our hands are all enmeshed
a circle beyond all boundaries.
Let us find the way to peace
and the gladness of communion
in which the fractures from our strain
heal up in resolution.
May we make a banquet spread
with giving enough for plenty
mouths and minds all to be fed
and every spirit strong.
Help me live and I'll help you
we'll build a world together
weaving of our threads of light
a great and gorgeous pillar.

in celebration of the Tuttles

Apotheosis

The valley turned me
    on to yellow
you turned me on to you
the sound of light
the song of the void
whispering messages
    heard forever before
the pool of a love
the strength of a tree
the endless knowing
    of a heart that's free.

Weather within, weather without
calm as galactic summer sea
    great the day child led
    shaman to ceremony
and one another's childs
knowing without believing, and believing
    because, well, that's what people do.
The valley turned me on to yellow,
you were you.

1993

to Megan Peters

Delivered

Were we to walk beside the mountain stream
swift weaving shadows in and out of light
shoulders screens of flickering incidence
where sun's searching rays insinuate

the whole of life would seem a blinking craze
an epilepsy, seizing naught to stay

but that our eyes hold upon the forms
whose movement 'neath masquerade remain
silhouettes between the boughs' charades
spirits traipsing, self-possessing flames

the world would be a dizzied stage
if not for characters' continuation

the light upon the flowing water's change
plays imitating like the spirits' phasing
slights of truth in life unwavering
within the coursing rivulets one force cascading

the hope within our hearts depends
on knowing meanings make one end

what acts against our purposes meeting
wreaks havoc to cosmic entreaty
of unity falling to a state of states
creating fleeing personalities of a face

perversity is vision cracked
eyes lost to see creation

yet the rivers flow into the sea
on land, rains preciously gather
all the shifting shapes agree
taking place upon a pattern

surface schemes can betray our love
this reverse is magic blackened
but these moments are dead, shed like skin
and organic sight is gladdened.

1999q

Moments of Tao

for Huai Shuen Feng
on her "25th" birthday

THE BOY'S TEETH CHATTERED like frightened candy as his eyes darted again down the quiet street.

While he waited for the sight of his mother's minivan, Raymond tugged on his coat sleeves, trying to pull the ends over his hands, managing only to clasp at the sleeve ends with his fingers doggedly. Again he stuffed his hands away by crossing his arms. His heel kicked at the granite sidewalk more to make a distraction than because of any.

He'd waited 20 minutes past the time his mother said she would come. Why hadn't she told him just to get a ride with the Matthews? No. She would come. "I can come get you," she said. He should have told her not to bother. "I can go with Jerry," are the words he should have forced off his tongue. But he hadn't, not wanting to indicate he doubted her.

Of course he was cautious not to show his doubt for the very reason that he did doubt her. It wasn't a concern about her feelings so much, though he admitted with resignation that was part of it, but a greater concern for avoiding the conversation that would come from showing his doubt.

"Don't you think I'll come get you?" she would say indignantly. "You think I'm gonna leave you there? You think I don't love you enough to pick up my son? Is that what I'm hearing?" On and on. Then on the ride home, a prisoner of that conversation. "You think I wasn't gonna come or some-thing? You think you have a room in the house but you're not my own family?"

She'd look at little Raymond incredul-ously, making her hurt into a tool of torture in this torture chamber of a vehicle. Once home he could quickly retreat to his privacy, but the trip home would be as oppressive as being buried alive. So he hadn't differed when she said she'd come. He'd chosen the easy way rather than the hard way. He'd learned to do that long ago.

Biting his chapped lip, he pondered pointlessly that he shouldn't know so much, or think so deeply, at his young age. I'm only twelve, he thought, glancing at the ruddy ends of his child's fingertips. What will I have to think about when I'm older? The street was still empty. The light was oddly pale.

It's not really that cold, he considered attentively. More cold on the inside than the outside, he managed to muse bitterly. Bitterness was an old companion, but sardonicism, a feeling for which he had no words, was newer to him. He wasn't sure if it was healthy to make light of his pain.

He started to walk along the route she'd likely take, if she did come at all. "What? You couldn't wait for me?" he heard her jagged voice piercing his ears. "You think I wasn't coming? Is that what you thought?" If only someone would pay him to do impressions of his mother. He could do that very well, he reflected with a touch of pride.

Piercing his ears. He traced back to the thought while he walked. That was a cool idea. Maybe just little black rings or something. No big hanging thing like Richie's! He smiled and felt the rhythm of his stride, his slight frame bobbing through the air. His mother would oppose it, but he could wear her down. Lots of kids had them. What could she do, play the meanie so blatantly? He could cause her enough grief over it that she'd relent to save herself the trouble.

"It's not me they're gonna call 'girlie,'" she'd say. Did they ever, he wondered briefly. Seemed like a thicket of an idea. He walked on, watching his breath.

Turning left at Darlington, the gray house on the corner extended down the block a ways. The white window frames had trails of dirt along the trim. Would look a lot better clean. Who's letting things slide in that house? he chided mentally. He ran his finger on an edge as he passed. Dirty! he observed more consciously. But it doesn't take a whole lot of dirt to make something dirty, is what he concluded from the thin film that held to the paint.

Against a fence dividing a driveway from the next property, a Big Wheel sat at rest. How long had it been there? Did a child leave it there carefully or just tire of it? A small park was up ahead on the left. No one there. That pale light. The grass seemed to crouch close to the ground. Swings hung limply and the slide and sandbox only echoed of activity that wasn't likely very recent.

A wrought iron fence at the far side of the park kept people from slipping off a steep grade, he knew. Trash accumulated past the fence, he saw in recollection. Is the whole world a trash can, for pete's sake? Would he be like his mother one day, he ruminated. Was he like her already without knowing it? He stiffened to the trash unseen down the grade, and to the thought he'd just entertained.

Nearing some benches perpendicular to the road, facing a dry fountain, he did notice a small seated figure. As he passed he looked to see a face, the back of the head wrapped in a scarf. "Hi," he said reflexively, seeing an Asian woman who looked neither tired nor sad.

"Hi," she answered, interjecting warmth in the cold air between them.

"Aren't you freezing out here?" he asked in response to her greeting.

"Is it cold? I thought just air maybe old." She laughed a little at her joke. Her eyes danced like the flames of two candles. She was sitting in a posture against the cold, but she didn't seem to *be* cold. Like it was a different season inside her.

What she'd said registered as odd but also intriguing. He slowed his step just long enough for her to enjoin, "Why don't you sit down here where temperature is better?" She was still beaming a playful smile and he thought, why not? This lady isn't going to hurt me or anything.

He sat on the bench a few feet from her and noticed her slightly worn-looking white, knitted gloves. Her hands were on her lap. "Do you think this fountain is working in summertime?" she asked him in a cheerful manner. Her speech was complicated by her accent, Chinese he assumed. But her words flowed on a sweet spirit that made her easy to understand.

"Yeah, it works," Raymond told her. "In the summer they turn it on." He wasn't sure why he'd sat down to talk with the woman. A small black bird stepped around undisturbed by the base of the fountain. Was he the bird, Raymond thought, aimless in the woman's company, or was she the bird, who met the day unruffled by the conditions around her? "That's good," she responded. "I like the fountain."

Raymond turned a little bit more to face her. He couldn't really tell how old she was. "Where are you from?" he asked curiously.

"From Taiwan," she said with strength in her voice. "You know where it is?"

"It's near China, right?"

"You're smart boy. Taiwan is used to be part of China."

Raymond still sought clues to get a clearer impression of the woman, but his glances seemed not to catch her, like water running on glass. "Why are you sitting here?" he finally asked plainly, stammering a little.

Now she turned her head toward him and looked into his eyes. She appeared to him to be wise, but not the worse for it. It was somewhat mysterious to him how she held her knowledge without being weighed down by it, as if it were light. "Why don't I be bird and fly away? This bench not good?"

"I guess it's okay," Raymond had to answer. "But you're out here by yourself."

"No, I'm not!" she said merrily.

"I mean you were," he corrected himself, while also appreciating her adeptness in their interchange.

"No. Sky is here. Bird is here. All sitting together." She smiled in a way that said, "Maybe that's hard for you to understand."

"The sky is always there. The bird doesn't talk to you. I don't get it." Raymond shook his head to show he knew he was missing something.

"True, sky always there," she nodded, continuing. "But sky is there now. That's important part. That's what mean something in now time. Bird talk too, very quiet." She raised her eyebrows as if to say the bird had told her secrets.

"What do you mean? The bird *talks*?" Raymond tried his best to use a New York City tone of disbelief.

"Well, maybe I talk more." She laughed more heartily and shrugged slightly. "Bird is telling me be here for the child to come."

"No." But rather than argue with her about that nonsense point, he thought better of it and simply replied, "Well, the bird must like you. He stays nearby."

"That's sweet for you to say," she returned softly. "You stay too."

Again Raymond wondered why he was sitting here talking to the woman. "I just thought you needed someone to talk to," he offered, passing off his own loneliness.

"Oh, so nice of you talk to me." She smiled warmly again and they sat for some moments. "Bird tell me you like talk to someone too."

Raymond looked quizzically at the bird. "No. The bird didn't tell you that."

"Bird tell me you no want to be walking this way." The woman looked for confirmation.

Raymond looked again at the bird, his head falling to one side. "What's that bird gonna tell you next," he exclaimed in a mutter.

"But no problem. Bird no know everything." The woman pressed down the long coat against her lap. "Bird tell me sometimes not true." She smiled at Raymond for forgiveness.

"Did that bird tell you when my mother's gonna come?" Raymond asked then with a bit of defiance.

"She'll come," the woman assured him. "Mother is coming."

"You don't know my mother," Raymond said with the confidence that this time he was the one who knew something.

The woman nodded slowly in acquiescence. "I don't know your mother."

Raymond's eyes tightened a little as he looked at the stone fountain. "That's what my mother's like," he pointed at the fountain. Sharing with the stranger what he had never dared utter in his life, he said quietly and a bit plaintively, "She's all stone and no water."

The woman was visibly surprised. "That's sad for you tell me that." Something in her seemed broken suddenly. "Do you really feel that way?" she asked with a little pain from the broken spot.

"She's hard as a rock," he looked straight forward and swallowed hard. He blinked away the onset of tears.

"Maybe you don't look so straight at things. Look solid, but not."

Raymond looked at her like she was going to tell another bird story.

She continued. "Things not solid as they look. But when you looking at them too straight," she pointed the fingers of her hand together, "look solid."

"It's solid," Raymond gestured to the fountain.

"No. Half solid, half air."

"It's solid." He got up and kicked the fountain, then turned to face her in a bit of a slump.

"No. Half solid, half air. Your solid part kicks fountain solid part."

"Where's the air?" Raymond poked his index finger against the heel of his other hand.

"Your mind," she pointed at her head, "half awake, still half sleeping. Only awake part sees solid, only asleep part sees air." She observed him tentatively. "You see solid with your awake mind." She patted the bench for reference.

"Everything's air when you sleep, and just solid when you're awake?" Raymond still stood facing her, his slump now more hardened.

"No. Then it's turn around. Then everything half air, half solid." She smiled hopefully. "Dreaming seems like all air but really half solid too."

"How are dreams half solid?" He was at least enjoying having a spirited argument. Time felt real.

"In dream, you don't look straight at things, feels more solid, right? When you awake, don't look straight at something, feels more like dream. Right?"

Raymond scratched his head. "Don't look straight at it?" he gestured again at the fountain skeptically.

"Look, but not so straight. Still see, but see half solid, half air."

Raymond seemed to break out of his slump, yet didn't straighten his posture. A quirky sound that he took to be a laugh came from the woman, and though he couldn't tell her age, he could tell that in some way she was still very young. He shuffled back to the bench and sat.

"How old are you?" he asked, as if that information would make everything clear. She looked him in the eyes again and said nothing. He figured only women getting on in years don't tell their age. "If you're 25, that's still not that old."

She smiled and nodded, accepting his wisdom.

A minivan went by that caught Raymond's attention. "Mom! Mom!" he ran after it. The bird flew off in the other direction. Finally the driver braked and stopped.

"Why aren't you where you're supposed to be?" she snapped.

Raymond turned to the woman on the bench, who was looking over her shoulder toward him. Still he didn't have a clear sense of the woman. But he waved goodbye, as did she, and for the briefest moment he thought he'd seen the fountain flowing.

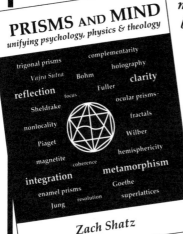

what's been said about *Prisms and Mind*

"A very different framework... Here is
a thread and an understanding that brings
wholeness to all we experience and know."

The New Times

"A concentrated meditation on prisms
as a metaphor for understanding patterns
in the physical world and in relation to
consciousness. Advances an intuitive view
of science ... the fruit of much thought
and reading."

Scientific & Medical Network Review

"A gem of a book that will illuminate
the reader's life."

Stanley Krippner, Ph. D.
noted author

"*Prisms and Mind* presents a synthesis of
ancient wisdom and contemporary science
that opens doorways to understanding of
both inner and outer reality. Building on
the author's central discovery of the
prismatic nature of consciousness, the book
reveals an ever-deepening interconnectedness
and meaning."

Will Tuttle, Ph.D.
educator, concert pianist, recording artist

in physical science

(from Rutter) As cooling metals solidify, a prismatic substructure is formed.

(from Benimoff) "Scanning electron microscopy reveals the presence of hexagonal prisms."

(from Degraff) Even igneous rock, the basic rock type, has prismatic structural characteristics.

(from Graber-Brunner) Gravity fields have been theorized to have prismatic attributes.

and much, much more...

in philosophy

From Eastern theological texts, such as the *Vajra Sutra* or *Diamond Sutra*, to those in the West—Christensen's syntactic analyses of the Old Testament; Pfisterer's *Prism of Scripture*—we find the prismatic nature of "parts of wholes" to be elemental. Prismatic themes are ubiquitous, from Rigg's "theory of prismatic society"; to Bucky Fuller's "geometry of thinking"; to Talbot's *Holographic Universe*, and Young's *Geometry of Meaning*.

As A. Govinda, author of *Foundations of Tibetan Mysticism*, says: "He who has found the Philosopher's Stone, the radiant jewel of the enlightened mind within his own heart, transforms his mortal consciousness into that of immortality, perceives the infinite in the finite and turns *Samsara* into *Nirvana*."

carbon are we, from coal to diamond do we evolve

First a poem calls to you,
Then you need it.

TIME
IS A
BROKEN
CARAFE

writings by Zach Shatz

more poetry
by the author of
WORDSWORD

Time is a
Broken Carafe

50 pp., $5.00
ISBN 1-892814-00-5

In a cornucopia of poetic styles,
from highly formal sonnet forms to trenchant
free verse, the author explores the concepts of
identity, discovery and the transmuting of
innocence. Deft, cathartic and evocative.

1986, perfect-bound

order direct: $6.20 incl. shipping
(Check or money order only, $US,
$7.00 outside U.S.A.)

PRISMIND Publications
Box 11635, Berkeley CA 94712

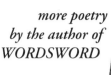
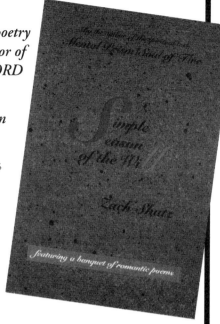

Prismind Publications
package offers

- *any 2 books – retail total only, shipping charges paid*
  (outside USA add $2)

- *any 3 books – $15 total*
  (outside USA add $3)

Thank you!

PRISMIND
PUBLICATIONS
P.O. Box 11635
Berkeley CA 94712